ONE POT

Contents

Welcome!

Not only am I a dedicated and enthusiastic cook, but I love nothing more than encouraging those who think they are domestically challenged to pick up a pan and a spoon and get stirring. It doesn't take much to grasp the basics and from there, anything is possible. Hiding behind the mantra 'I can't cook' only brings fear into the kitchen, but it is these mistakes that will ultimately make you a better, more confident and knowledgeable cook. All it takes is some good recipes and plenty of enthusiasm and kitchen domination will surely follow. Luckily, all Good Housekeeping cookery books are filled with tempting recipes with clear methods and realistic photography – we are taking the chance out of cooking as our recipes are guaranteed to work.

If you have ever tried turning the page of a cookery book with dirty hands, while also balancing a steaming pan and a sticky spoon, then you will love the flip-chart design of this book. The simple fact that the recipes stand upright makes for an easier cooking experience – say goodbye to hovering over recipes while trying to stop the spoon dripping on to the pages.

This Good Housekeeping Flip It! book collection is filled with meticulously triple-tested recipes that have been developed and put through their paces in our dedicated test kitchens. We hope you enjoy the recipes and that they inspire you to give them a try – you know that they'll work after all!

Meike.

Cookery Editor
Good Housekeeping

Spicy Bean & Courgette Soup

Serves 4
Preparation Time
10 minutes
Cooking Time
30 minutes

Per Serving
289 calories
8g fat
(of which 1g saturates)
43g carbohydrate
1.5g salt

Vegetarian Dairy Free

2 tbsp olive oil
175g (6oz) onions, finely chopped
2 garlic cloves, crushed
2 tsp ground coriander
1 tbsp paprika
1 tsp mild curry powder
450g (1lb) courgettes, trimmed, halved and sliced
225g (8oz) potatoes, diced
400g can red kidney beans, drained and rinsed
425g can flageolet beans, drained and rinsed
1.5 litres (2½ pints) vegetable stock
salt and ground black pepper
crusty bread to serve

1 Heat the oil in a pan. Add the onions and garlic and sauté for 2 minutes. Add the spices and cook, stirring, for 1 minute. Mix in the courgettes and potatoes and cook for 1-2 minutes.

2 Add the remaining ingredients and bring to the boil, then reduce the heat, cover the pan and simmer for 25 minutes, stirring occasionally, or until the potatoes are tender. Adjust the seasoning if necessary.

3 Ladle into warmed bowls and serve with crusty bread.

Cook's Tip
Courgettes are baby marrows. Look for small firm vegetables. They lose their flavour as they grow larger.

Smoked Cod & Sweetcorn Chowder

Serves 6
Preparation Time
5 minutes
Cooking Time
20 minutes

Per Serving
517 calories
28g fat
(of which 15g saturates)
35g carbohydrate
4.7g salt

130g pack cubed pancetta
50g (2oz) butter
3 leeks, about 450g (1lb), trimmed and thinly sliced
25g (1oz) plain flour
600ml (1 pint) semi-skimmed or full-fat milk
700g (1½lb) undyed smoked cod loin or haddock,
skinned and cut into 2cm (¾in) cubes
326g can sweetcorn in water, drained
450g (1lb) small new potatoes, sliced
150ml (¼ pint) double cream
½ tsp paprika
salt and ground black pepper
2 tbsp freshly chopped flat-leafed parsley to garnish

1 Fry the pancetta in a large pan over a gentle heat until the fat runs out. Add the butter to the pan to melt, then add the leeks and cook until softened.

2 Stir in the flour and cook for a few seconds, then pour in the milk and 300ml (½ pint) cold water. Add the fish to the pan with the sweetcorn and potato. Bring to the boil, reduce the heat and simmer for 10–15 minutes until the potatoes are cooked.

3 Stir in the cream, season with salt and pepper and the paprika, and cook for 2–3 minutes to warm through. Ladle into warmed shallow bowls and sprinkle each one with a little chopped parsley. Serve immediately.

Full-of-goodness Broth

Serves 4
Preparation Time
10 minutes
Cooking Time
6–8 minutes

Per Serving
107 calories
4g fat
(of which trace
saturates)
9g carbohydrate
1g salt

**Vegetarian Gluten
Free Dairy Free**

1–2 tbsp medium curry paste (see Cook's Tip)
200ml (7fl oz) reduced-fat coconut milk
600ml (1 pint) hot vegetable stock
200g (7oz) smoked tofu, cubed
2 pak choi, chopped
a handful of sugarsnap peas
4 spring onions, chopped
lime wedges to serve

1 Heat the curry paste in a pan for 1–2 minutes. Add the coconut milk and hot stock, and bring to the boil.

2 Add the smoked tofu cubes, chopped pak choi, sugarsnap peas and spring onions. Reduce the heat and simmer for 1–2 minutes.

3 Ladle into warmed bowls and serve with a wedge of lime to squeeze over the broth.

Try Something Different
Replace the smoked tofu with shredded leftover roast chicken and simmer for 2–3 minutes.

Cook's Tip
Check the ingredients in the curry paste: some may not be suitable for vegetarians.

Thai Chicken Broth

Serves 4
Preparation Time
20 minutes
Cooking Time
20-25 minutes

Per Serving
198 calories
5g fat
(of which 1g saturates)
13g carbohydrate
1.1g salt

Dairy Free

1 tbsp olive oil
4 boneless skinless
chicken thighs, around
300g (11oz), shredded
3 garlic cloves,
roughly chopped
2 red chillies, seeded
and finely diced (see
Cook's Tips)
1 lemongrass stalk,
finely sliced
5cm (2in) piece of
fresh root ginger,
finely chopped
150ml (¼ pint)
white wine

1 litre (1¾ pints)
chicken stock
8 fresh coriander sprigs
50g (2oz) rice noodles
125g (4oz) green
beans, trimmed
and halved
125g (4oz) bean sprouts
4 spring onions,
finely sliced
2 tbsp Thai fish sauce
(nam pla)
juice of ½ lime
salt and ground black
pepper

1 Heat the oil in a large pan over a medium heat. Add the chicken, garlic, chillies, lemongrass and ginger, and cook for 3-5 minutes until the chicken is opaque.

2 Add the wine, bring to the boil, lower the heat and simmer until reduced by half. Add the stock and bring to the boil, then reduce the heat and simmer for 5 minutes or until the chicken is cooked through.

3 Pick the leaves off the coriander and put them to one side. Finely chop the coriander stalks. Add the noodles to the pan and cook for 1 minute, then add the beans and coriander stalks. Cook for 3 minutes.

4 Add the bean sprouts and spring onions (reserving a few to garnish) along with the fish sauce and lime juice. Bring to the boil and taste for seasoning. Ladle the noodles and broth into four warmed bowls, making sure that each serving has some chicken and bean sprouts. Garnish with the coriander leaves, spring onions and bean sprouts and serve.

Cook's Tips
Chillies vary enormously in strength, from quite mild to blisteringly hot, depending on the type of chilli and its ripeness. Taste a small piece first to check it's not too hot for you.
Be extremely careful when handling chillies not to touch or rub your eyes with your fingers, as they will sting. Wash knives immediately after handling chillies for the same reason. As a precaution, use rubber gloves when preparing them if you like.

Seafood Gumbo

Serves 4
Preparation Time
10 minutes
Cooking Time
30 minutes

Per Serving
559 calories
23g fat
(of which 3g saturates)
58g carbohydrate
1.2g salt

125g (4oz) butter
50g (2oz) plain flour
1–2 tbsp Cajun spice mix
1 onion, chopped
1 green pepper, seeded and chopped
5 spring onions, sliced
1 tbsp freshly chopped flat-leafed parsley
1 garlic clove, crushed
1 beef tomato, chopped
125g (4oz) garlic sausage, finely sliced
75g (3oz) American easy-cook rice

1.1 litres (2 pints) vegetable stock
450g (1lb) okra, sliced
1 bay leaf
1 fresh thyme sprig
2 tsp salt
¼ tsp cayenne pepper
juice of ½ lemon
4 cloves
500g (1lb 2oz) frozen mixed seafood (containing mussels, squid and prawns), thawed and drained
ground black pepper

1 Heat the butter in a 2.5 litre (4¼–4½ pint) heavy-based pan over a low heat. Add the flour and Cajun spice and cook, stirring, for 1–2 minutes until golden brown. Add the onion, green pepper, spring onions, parsley and garlic. Cook for 5 minutes.

2 Add the tomato, garlic sausage and rice to the pan and stir well to coat. Add the stock, okra, bay leaf, thyme, salt, cayenne pepper, lemon juice and cloves. Season with black pepper. Bring to the boil, then reduce the heat and simmer, covered, for 12 minutes or until the rice is tender.

3 Add the seafood and cook for 2 minutes to heat through. Serve the gumbo in deep bowls.

Cook's Tip
Gumbo is a traditional stew from the southern states of the USA, containing meat, vegetables and shellfish and thickened with okra.

Spinach & Rice Soup

Serves 4

Preparation Time

10 minutes

Cooking Time

25-30 minutes

Per Serving

335 calories

20g fat

(of which 4g saturates)

29g carbohydrate

0.7g salt

Gluten Free

4 tbsp extra virgin olive oil, plus extra to serve

1 onion, finely chopped

2 garlic cloves, crushed

2 tsp freshly chopped thyme or a large pinch
of dried thyme

2 tsp freshly chopped rosemary or a large pinch
of dried rosemary

zest of ½ lemon

2 tsp ground coriander

¼ tsp cayenne pepper

125g (4oz) arborio rice

1.1 litres (2 pints) vegetable stock

225g (8oz) fresh or frozen and thawed spinach, shredded

4 tbsp fresh pesto (see Cook's Tip)

salt and ground black pepper

freshly grated Parmesan to serve

1 Heat half the oil in a pan. Add the onion, garlic, herbs, lemon zest and spices, then fry gently for 5 minutes.

2 Add the remaining oil with the rice and cook, stirring, for 1 minute. Add the stock and bring to the boil, then reduce the heat and simmer gently for 20 minutes or until the rice is tender.

3 Stir the spinach into the soup with the pesto. Cook for 2 minutes, then season to taste with salt and pepper.

4 Ladle into warmed bowls and serve drizzled with a little oil and topped with Parmesan.

Cook's Tip

Fresh Pesto To make fresh pesto roughly tear 50g (2oz) fresh basil leaves and put it into a mortar with 1-2 peeled garlic cloves, 25g (1oz) pinenuts and a little extra virgin olive oil (you will need 6 tbsp in total). Pound with a pestle to a paste. Alternatively, work in a food processor to a fairly smooth paste. Gradually work in the rest of the oil and season with salt and pepper to taste. Transfer to a bowl. Stir in 2 tbsp freshly grated Parmesan, check the seasoning and add a squeeze of lemon juice, if you like. Store in a screw-topped jar, covered with a thin layer of oil, in the fridge for up to three days. Serves 4.

Chicken & Bean Soup

Serves 4

Preparation Time
10 minutes

Cooking Time
30 minutes

Per Serving
351 calories
6g fat
(of which 1g saturates)
48g carbohydrate
2.7g salt

Dairy Free

1 tbsp olive oil
1 onion, finely chopped
4 celery sticks, chopped
1 red chilli, seeded and roughly chopped
(see Cook's Tips, page 10)
2 boneless, skinless chicken breasts,
about 125g (4oz) each, cut into strips
1 litre (1¾ pints) hot chicken or vegetable stock
100g (3½oz) bulgur wheat
2 × 400g cans cannellini beans, drained and rinsed
400g can chopped tomatoes
25g (1oz) flat-leafed parsley, roughly chopped
salt and ground black pepper
wholegrain bread and hummus to serve

1 Heat the oil in a large heavy-based pan. Add the onion, celery and chilli and cook over a low heat for 10 minutes or until softened. Add the chicken and stir-fry for 3–4 minutes until golden.

2 Add the hot stock to the pan and bring to a simmer. Stir in the bulgur wheat and simmer for 15 minutes.

3 Stir in the cannellini beans and tomatoes and bring to a simmer. Check the seasoning. Ladle into four warmed bowls and sprinkle with chopped parsley. Serve with wholegrain bread and hummus.

Thai Noodles with Prawns

Serves 4

Preparation Time
10 minutes

Cooking Time
5 minutes

Per Serving
343 calories
11g fat
(of which 2g saturates)
40g carbohydrate
1g salt

Dairy Free

4–6 tsp Thai red curry paste
175g (6oz) medium egg noodles
(wholewheat if possible)
2 small red onions, chopped
1 lemongrass stalk, trimmed
and sliced
1 fresh red bird's-eye chilli, seeded and
finely chopped (see Cook's Tips, page 10)
300ml (½ pint) reduced-fat
coconut milk
400g (14oz) raw tiger prawns, peeled and
deveined (see Cook's Tip)
4 tbsp freshly chopped coriander, plus
extra freshly torn coriander to garnish
salt and ground black pepper

1 Pour 2 litres (3½ pints) water into a large pan and
bring to the boil. Add the curry paste, noodles,
onions, lemongrass, chilli and coconut milk and bring
back to the boil.

2 Add the prawns and chopped coriander, reduce the
heat and simmer for 2–3 minutes until the prawns
turn pink. Season with salt and pepper.

3 To serve, divide the noodles among four large bowls
and sprinkle with the torn coriander.

Cook's Tip
To peel and devein prawns, pull off the head and discard
(or put to one side and use later for making stock). Using
pointed scissors, cut through the soft shell on the belly
side. Prise off the shell, leaving the tail attached. (The
shell can also be used later for making stock.) Using a
small sharp knife, make a shallow cut along the back of
the prawn. Using the point of the knife, remove and
discard the black vein (the intestinal tract) that runs
along the back of the prawn.

Baked Tomatoes & Fennel

Serves 6
Preparation Time
10 minutes
Cooking Time
1¼ hours

Per Serving
127 calories
9g fat
(of which 1g saturates)
7g carbohydrate
0.1g salt

**Vegetarian Gluten
Free Dairy Free**

900g (2lb) fennel, trimmed and cut into quarters
75ml (2½fl oz) white wine
5 thyme sprigs
75ml (2½fl oz) olive oil
900g (2lb) ripe beef or plum tomatoes
salt and ground black pepper

1 Preheat the oven to 200°C (180°C fan oven) mark 6.
Put the fennel into a roasting tin and pour the white
wine over it. Snip the thyme sprigs over the fennel,
drizzle with the oil and season. Roast for 45 minutes.

2 Halve the tomatoes, add to the roasting tin and
continue to roast for 30 minutes or until tender,
basting with the juices halfway through.

Cook's Tip
This is an ideal accompaniment to grilled fish or meat, or
a vegetarian frittata.

Warm Spiced Rice Salad

Serves 4	½ tbsp ground cumin
Preparation Time	½ tsp ground cinnamon
10 minutes	2 tbsp sunflower oil
Cooking Time	2 large red onions, sliced
20-30 minutes	250g (9oz) basmati rice
	600ml (1 pint) hot vegetable or chicken stock
Per Serving	400g can lentils, drained and rinsed
700 calories	salt and ground black pepper
27g fat	
(of which 6g saturates)	**For the salad**
88g carbohydrate	75g (3oz) watercress
0.7g salt	250g (9oz) broccoli, steamed and chopped into 2.5cm (1in) pieces
Vegetarian	25g (1oz) sultanas
Gluten Free	75g (3oz) dried apricots, chopped
	75g (3oz) mixed nuts and seeds
	2 tbsp freshly chopped flat-leafed parsley
	100g (3½oz) goat's cheese, crumbled

1 Put the cumin and cinnamon into a large deep frying pan and heat gently for 1–2 minutes. Add the oil and onions and fry over a low heat for 8–10 minutes until the onions are soft. Add the rice, toss to coat in the spices and onions, then add the hot stock. Cover and cook for 12–15 minutes until the stock has been absorbed and the rice is cooked. Season, tip into a serving bowl and add the lentils.

2 To make the salad, add the watercress, broccoli, sultanas, apricots and mixed nuts and seeds to the bowl. Scatter with the parsley, then toss together, top with the cheese and serve immediately.

Try Something Different
Replace the goat's cheese with two roasted, skinless chicken breasts, which have been shredded.

Spicy Squash Quarters

Serves 8
Preparation Time
10 minutes
Cooking Time
20–30 minutes

Per Serving
97 calories
8g fat
(of which 5g saturates)
4g carbohydrate
0.1g salt

Vegetarian
Gluten Free

2 small butternut squash, quartered and seeds discarded
75g (3oz) butter, melted
4 tsp peppered steak seasoning
coarse sea salt to sprinkle
wild rocket to serve

1 Preheat the grill or barbecue to medium-hot. Sprinkle the squash with sea salt, brush with butter and sprinkle the steak seasoning over.

2 Cook the squash quarters for 20–30 minutes until tender, turning them over occasionally. Serve hot, with wild rocket.

Try Something Different
Instead of the steak seasoning, lightly toast 2 tsp coriander seeds. Roughly crush and stir into the melted butter before brushing on to the squash. When cooked, toss with fresh coriander leaves.

Roasted Ratatouille

Serves 6
Preparation Time
15 minutes
Cooking Time
1½ hours

Per Serving
224 calories
18g fat
(of which 3g saturates)
14g carbohydrate
0g salt

Vegetarian Gluten
Free Dairy Free

400g (14oz) red peppers, seeded
and roughly chopped
700g (1½lb) aubergines, stalk
removed, cut into chunks
450g (1lb) onions, peeled and cut
into wedges
4 or 5 garlic cloves, unpeeled and
left whole
150ml (¼ pint) olive oil
1 tsp fennel seeds
200ml (7fl oz) passata
sea salt and ground black pepper
a few fresh thyme sprigs to garnish

1 Preheat the oven to 240°C (220°C fan oven) mark 9. Put the peppers, aubergine, onions, garlic, oil and fennel seeds in a roasting tin. Season with sea salt flakes and pepper, and toss together.

2 Transfer to the oven and cook for 30 minutes (tossing frequently during cooking) or until the vegetables are charred and beginning to soften.

3 Stir the passata through the vegetables, and put the roasting tin back in the oven for 50–60 minutes, stirring occasionally. Garnish with the thyme sprigs and serve.

Try Something Different
Replace half the aubergines with 400g (14oz) courgettes; use a mix of green and red peppers; garnish with fresh basil instead of thyme.

Stir-fried Green Vegetables

Serves 6

Preparation Time
5 minutes

Cooking Time
3-4 minutes

Per Serving
100 calories
8g fat
(of which 3g saturates)
5g carbohydrate
0.1g salt

Vegetarian
Gluten Free

2 tbsp vegetable oil
225g (8oz) courgettes, thinly sliced
175g (6oz) mangetouts
25g (1oz) butter
175g (6oz) frozen peas, thawed
salt and ground black pepper

1 Heat the oil in a wok or large frying pan, add the courgettes and stir-fry for 1–2 minutes. Add the mangetouts and cook for 1 minute. Add the butter and peas and cook for 1 minute. Season to taste with salt and pepper and serve immediately.

Try Something Different
Try other vegetables, such as thinly sliced leeks, spring onions or pak choi.

Black-eye Bean Chilli

Serves 4
Preparation Time
10 minutes
Cooking Time
20 minutes

Per Serving
245 calories
5g fat
(of which 1g saturates)
39g carbohydrate
1.8g salt

Vegetarian

1 tbsp olive oil
1 onion, chopped
3 celery sticks, finely chopped
2 × 400g cans black-eye beans, drained
and rinsed
2 × 400g cans chopped tomatoes
2 or 3 splashes of Tabasco sauce
3 tbsp freshly chopped coriander
warm tortillas and soured cream to serve

1 Heat the olive oil in a heavy-based frying pan over a low heat. Add the onion and celery, and fry for 10 minutes until softened.

2 Add the black-eye beans to the pan with the tomatoes and Tabasco sauce. Bring to the boil, then reduce the heat and simmer for 10 minutes.

3 Just before serving, stir in the chopped coriander. Spoon the chilli on to warm tortillas, and serve with a spoonful of soured cream.

Try Something Different
Replace half the black-eye beans with red kidney beans.

Pan-fried Chorizo & Potato

Serves 4
Preparation Time
10 minutes
Cooking Time
30 minutes

Per Serving
553 calories
36g fat
(of which 12g saturates)
32g carbohydrate
3.4g salt

Gluten Free Dairy Free

2 tbsp olive oil
450g (1lb) potatoes, cut into 2.5cm
(1in) cubes
2 red onions, sliced
1 red pepper, seeded and chopped
1 tsp paprika
300g (11oz) piece of chorizo sausage,
skinned and cut into chunky slices
250g (9oz) cherry tomatoes
100ml (3½fl oz) dry sherry
2 tbsp freshly chopped flat-leafed parsley

1 Heat the oil in a large heavy-based frying pan over
a medium heat. Add the potatoes and fry for 7–10
minutes until lightly browned, turning regularly.

2 Reduce the heat, add the onions and red pepper, and
continue to cook for 10 minutes, stirring from time
to time, until they have softened but not browned.

3 Add the paprika and chorizo sausage and cook for
5 minutes, stirring from time to time.

4 Add the cherry tomatoes and pour in the sherry.
Stir everything together and cook for 5 minutes
until the sherry has reduced and the tomatoes have
softened and warmed through.

5 Sprinkle the chopped parsley over the top and serve.

Chilli Vegetable & Coconut Stir-fry

Serves 4
Preparation Time
25 minutes
Cooking Time
about 10 minutes

Per Serving
220 calories
12g fat
(of which 2g saturates)
22g carbohydrate
1.7g salt

Vegetarian Dairy Free

2 tbsp sesame oil
2 green chillies, seeded and chopped (see Cook's Tips, page 10)
2.5cm (1in) piece fresh root ginger, grated
2 garlic cloves, crushed
1 tbsp Thai green curry paste (see Cook's Tip, page 9)
125g (4oz) carrot, cut into fine matchsticks
125g (4oz) baby sweetcorn, halved
125g (4oz) mangetouts, halved on the diagonal
2 large red peppers, finely sliced

2 small pak choi, quartered
4 spring onions, finely chopped
300ml (½ pint) coconut milk
2 tbsp peanut satay sauce
2 tbsp light soy sauce
1 tsp soft brown sugar
4 tbsp freshly chopped coriander, plus extra sprigs to garnish
ground black pepper
roasted peanuts to garnish
rice or noodles to serve

1 Heat the oil in a wok or large non-stick frying pan over a medium heat, and stir-fry the chillies, ginger and garlic for 1 minute. Add the curry paste and fry for a further 30 seconds.

2 Add the carrot, sweetcorn, mangetouts and red peppers. Stir-fry over a high heat for 3–4 minutes, then add the pak choi and spring onions. Cook, stirring, for a further 1–2 minutes.

3 Pour in the coconut milk, satay sauce, soy sauce and sugar. Season with pepper, bring to the boil and cook for 1–2 minutes, then add the chopped coriander. Garnish with the peanuts and coriander sprigs, and serve with rice or noodles.

Tomato & Butter Bean Stew

Serves 4
Preparation Time
10 minutes
Cooking Time
50–55 minutes

Per Serving
286 calories
8g fat
(of which 1g saturates)
41g carbohydrate
1.8g salt

Vegetarian Dairy Free

2 tbsp olive oil
1 onion, finely sliced
2 garlic cloves, finely chopped
2 large leeks, sliced
2 × 400g cans cherry tomatoes
2 × 400g cans butter beans, drained and rinsed
150ml (¼ pint) hot vegetable stock
1–2 tbsp balsamic vinegar
salt and ground black pepper

1 Preheat the oven to 180°C (160°C fan oven) mark 4. Heat the oil in a flameproof casserole over a medium heat. Add the onion and garlic, and cook for 10 minutes until golden and soft. Add the leeks and cook, covered, for 5 minutes.

2 Add the tomatoes, beans and hot stock, and season well with salt and pepper. Bring to the boil, then cover and cook in the oven for 35–40 minutes until the sauce has thickened. Remove from the oven, stir in the vinegar and spoon into warmed bowls.

Courgette & Parmesan Frittata

Serves 4
Preparation Time
10 minutes
Cooking Time
15 minutes

Per Serving
457 calories
38g fat
(of which 18g saturates)
5g carbohydrate
1.2g salt

Gluten Free

40g (1½oz) butter
1 small onion, finely sliced
225g (8oz) courgettes, finely sliced
6 medium eggs, beaten
25g (1oz) freshly grated Parmesan,
plus shavings to garnish
salt and ground black pepper
crusty bread to serve

1 Melt 25g (1oz) of the butter in an 18cm (7in) non-stick frying pan, and cook the onion until soft. Add the courgettes and fry gently for 5 minutes or until they begin to soften.

2 Preheat the grill. Add the remaining butter to the frying pan. Season the eggs with salt and pepper, and pour into the pan. Cook for 2–3 minutes until golden underneath and cooked around the edges.

3 Scatter the grated cheese over the frittata and put under the preheated grill for 1–2 minutes or until just set. Garnish with Parmesan shavings, cut the frittata into quarters and serve with crusty bread.

Try Something Different
Instead of courgettes use leftover boiled potatoes, cut into small cubes.

Curried Coconut & Vegetable Rice

Serves 6
Preparation Time
15 minutes
Cooking Time
30 minutes, plus
standing

Per Serving
413 calories
17g fat
(of which 2g saturates)
57g carbohydrate
0.4g salt

Vegetarian
Gluten Free Dairy Free

1 large aubergine, about 300g (11oz)
1 large butternut squash, about 500g (1lb 2oz),
peeled and seeded
250g (9oz) dwarf green beans, trimmed
100ml (3½fl oz) vegetable oil
1 large onion, chopped
1 tbsp black mustard seeds
3 tbsp korma paste (see Cook's Tip, page 9)
350g (12oz) basmati rice
400ml can coconut milk
200g (7oz) baby spinach leaves
salt and ground black pepper

1 Cut the aubergine and butternut squash into 2cm (¾in) cubes. Slice the green beans into 2cm (¾in) pieces.

2 Heat the oil in a large pan. Add the onion and cook for about 5 minutes or until a light golden colour. Add the mustard seeds and cook, stirring, until they begin to pop. Stir in the korma paste and cook for 1 minute.

3 Add the aubergine and cook, stirring, for 5 minutes. Add the butternut squash, beans, rice and 2 tsp salt, mixing well. Pour in the coconut milk and add 600ml (1 pint) water. Bring to the boil, then reduce the heat, cover the pan and simmer for 15–18 minutes.

4 When the rice and vegetables are cooked, remove the lid and put the spinach leaves on top. Cover and leave, off the heat, for 5 minutes. Gently stir the wilted spinach through the rice, check the seasoning and serve immediately.

Italian Bean Stew

Serves 4
Preparation time
15 minutes
Cooking time
15 minutes

Per serving
405 calories
10g fat
(of which 1g saturates)
35g carbohydrate
1.3g salt

1 tbsp olive oil
2 large shallots, finely sliced
2 medium carrots, finely diced
1 celery stick, finely diced
1.5 litres (2 pints 12fl oz) hot
vegetable stock
250g (9oz) asparagus,
cut into 2cm (¾in) lengths
75g (3oz) tiny soup pasta,
such as ditalini or stellete
2 × 400g cans flageolet beans,
drained and rinsed
2 tbsp fresh pesto to serve (see
Cook's Tip page 13)

1 Heat the oil in a large pan. Add the shallots and fry gently for 3 minutes or until softened but not coloured.

2 Add the carrots, celery and hot stock, and bring to the boil. Reduce the heat and simmer for 10 minutes. Add the asparagus and pasta and cook for a further 7 minutes.

3 Stir in the flageolet beans and heat for 2–3 minutes. Divide among the bowls and serve with a swirl of pesto on top.

Spiced Bean & Vegetable Stew

Serves 6
Preparation Time
15 minutes
Cooking Time
35 minutes

Per Serving
262 calories
7g fat
(of which 1g saturates)
44g carbohydrate
1.3g salt

Vegetarian
Gluten Free Dairy Free

3 tbsp olive oil
2 small onions, sliced
2 garlic cloves, crushed
1 tbsp sweet paprika
1 small dried red chilli, seeded
and finely chopped (see Cook's
Tips, page 10)
700g (1½lb) sweet potatoes,
peeled and cubed
700g (1½lb) pumpkin, peeled
and cut into chunks
125g (4oz) okra, trimmed
500g jar passata
400g can haricot or cannellini
beans, drained and rinsed
salt and ground black pepper

1 Heat the oil in a large heavy-based pan over a very
gentle heat. Add the onions and garlic, and cook for
5 minutes.

2 Stir in the paprika and chilli, and cook for 2 minutes,
then add the sweet potatoes, pumpkin, okra, passata
and 900ml (1½ pints) cold water. Season generously with
salt and pepper.

3 Cover the pan, bring to the boil, then reduce the heat
and simmer for 20 minutes until the vegetables are
tender. Add the beans, cook for 3 minutes to warm
through, then serve.

Try Something Different
Instead of the paprika, use 1 tsp each ground cumin
and ground coriander. Garnish with some freshly
chopped coriander.

Chickpea Curry

Serves 6

Preparation Time

20 minutes

Cooking Time

40–45 minutes

Per Serving

291 calories

8g fat

(of which 1g saturates)

46g carbohydrate

1.3g salt

Vegetarian

Gluten Free Dairy Free

2 tbsp vegetable oil

2 onions, finely sliced

2 garlic cloves, crushed

1 tbsp ground coriander

1 tsp mild chilli powder

1 tbsp black mustard seeds

2 tbsp tamarind paste

2 tbsp sun-dried tomato paste

750g (1lb 10oz) new potatoes, quartered

400g can chopped tomatoes

1 litre (1¾ pints) hot vegetable stock

250g (9oz) green beans, trimmed

2 × 400g cans chickpeas, drained and rinsed

2 tsp garam masala

salt and ground black pepper

1 Heat the oil in a pan and fry the onions for 10–15 minutes until golden – when they have a good colour they will add depth of flavour. Add the garlic, coriander, chilli, mustard seeds, tamarind paste and sun-dried tomato paste. Cook for 1–2 minutes until the aroma from the spices is released.

2 Add the potatoes and toss in the spices for 1–2 minutes. Add the tomatoes and hot stock, and season with salt and pepper. Cover and bring to the boil, then reduce the heat and simmer, half covered, for 20 minutes or until the potatoes are just cooked.

3 Add the beans and chickpeas, and continue to cook for 5 minutes or until the beans are tender and the chickpeas are warmed through. Stir in the garam masala and serve.

Cook's Tip

Tamarind paste has a very sharp, sour flavour and is widely used in Asian and South-east Asian cooking.

Moroccan Chickpea Stew

Serves 4
Preparation Time
10 minutes
Cooking Time
40 minutes

Per Serving
232 calories
9g fat
(of which 1g saturates)
29g carbohydrate
0.6g salt

Vegetarian Dairy Free

1 red pepper, halved and seeded
1 green pepper, halved and seeded
1 yellow pepper, halved and seeded
2 tbsp olive oil
1 onion, finely sliced
2 garlic cloves, crushed
1 tbsp harissa paste
2 tbsp tomato purée
½ tsp ground cumin
1 aubergine, diced
400g can chickpeas, drained and rinsed
450ml (¾ pint) vegetable stock
4 tbsp roughly chopped fresh flat-leafed parsley,
plus a few sprigs to garnish
salt and ground black pepper

1 Preheat the grill and lay the peppers, skin side up, on a baking sheet. Grill for around 5 minutes until the skin begins to blister and char. Put the peppers in a plastic bag, seal and put to one side for a few minutes. When cooled a little, peel off the skins and discard, then slice the peppers and put to one side.

2 Heat the oil in a large heavy-based frying pan over a low heat, add the onion and cook for 5–10 minutes until soft. Add the garlic, harissa, tomato purée and cumin, and cook for 2 minutes.

3 Add the peppers to the pan with the aubergine. Stir everything to coat evenly with the spices and cook for 2 minutes. Add the chickpeas and stock, season well with salt and pepper, and bring to the boil. Reduce the heat and simmer for 20 minutes.

4 Just before serving, stir the parsley through the chickpea stew. Serve in warmed bowls, garnished with parsley sprigs.

Mushroom & Bean Hotpot

Serves 6

Preparation Time
15 minutes

Cooking Time
30 minutes

Per Serving
280 calories
10g fat
(of which 1g saturates)
34g carbohydrate
1.3g salt

Vegetarian Dairy Free

3 tbsp olive oil
700g (1½lb) chestnut mushrooms,
roughly chopped
1 large onion, finely chopped
2 tbsp plain flour
2 tbsp mild curry paste (see
Cook's Tip, page 9)
150ml (¼ pint) dry white wine
400g can chopped tomatoes
2 tbsp sun-dried tomato paste
2 × 400g cans mixed beans,
drained and rinsed
3 tbsp mango chutney
3 tbsp roughly chopped fresh
coriander and mint

1 Heat the oil in a large pan over a low heat, and fry the mushrooms and onion until the onion is soft and dark golden. Stir in the flour and curry paste, then cook for 1–2 minutes before adding the wine, tomatoes, sun-dried tomato paste and beans.

2 Bring to the boil, then reduce the heat and simmer gently for 30 minutes or until most of the liquid has reduced. Stir in the chutney and herbs before serving.

Veggie Curry

Serves 1
Preparation Time
5 minutes
Cooking Time
12 minutes

Per Serving
468 calories
20g fat
(of which 3g saturates)
58g carbohydrate
1.4g salt

Vegetarian
Gluten Free Dairy Free

1 tbsp medium curry paste
(see Cook's Tip, page 9)
227g can chopped tomatoes
150ml (¼ pint) hot vegetable stock
200g (7oz) vegetables, such as broccoli,
courgettes and sugarsnap peas,
roughly chopped
½ × 400g can chickpeas,
drained and rinsed
griddled wholemeal pitta bread
and yogurt to serve

1 Heat the curry paste in a large heavy-based pan for
1 minute, stirring the paste to warm the spices. Add
the tomatoes and hot stock. Bring to the boil, then reduce
the heat to a simmer and add the vegetables. Simmer for
5–6 minutes until the vegetables are tender.

2 Stir in the chickpeas and heat for 1–2 minutes until
hot. Serve the vegetable curry with a griddled
wholemeal pitta and yogurt.

Mauritian Vegetable Curry

Serves 4
Preparation Time
15 minutes
Cooking Time
30 minutes

Per Serving
184 calories
11g fat
(of which 1g saturates)
18g carbohydrate
1.7g salt

Vegetarian Dairy Free

3 tbsp vegetable oil
1 onion, finely sliced
4 garlic cloves, crushed
2.5cm (1in) piece of fresh root ginger, grated
3 level tbsp medium curry powder
6 fresh curry leaves
150g (5oz) potato, peeled and cut into 1cm (½in) cubes
125g (4oz) aubergine, cut into 2cm (1in) sticks, 5mm (¼in) wide

150g (5oz) carrots, peeled and cut into 5mm (¼in) dice
900ml (1½ pints) vegetable stock
pinch of saffron threads
1 tsp salt
150g (5oz) green beans, trimmed
75g (3oz) frozen peas
ground black pepper
3 tbsp chopped fresh coriander to garnish
naan bread to serve

1 Heat the oil in a large heavy-based pan over a low heat. Add the onion and fry for 5–10 minutes until golden. Add the garlic, ginger, curry powder and curry leaves, and fry for a further minute.

2 Add the potato and aubergine to the pan and fry, stirring, for 2 minutes. Add the carrots, stock, saffron and salt. Season with plenty of pepper. Cover and cook for 10 minutes until the vegetables are almost tender.

3 Add the beans and peas to the pan and cook for a further 4 minutes. Sprinkle with the chopped coriander and serve with naan bread.

Get Ahead

To prepare ahead Complete the recipe, without the garnish, and chill quickly. Keep in the refrigerator for up to two days.
To use Put in a pan, cover and bring to the boil, then reduce the heat and simmer for 10–15 minutes. Complete the recipe.

Scallops with Ginger

Serves 4
Preparation Time
15 minutes
Cooking Time
3 minutes

Per Serving
197 calories
7g fat
(of which 1g saturates)
6g carbohydrate
2g salt

Dairy Free

2 tbsp vegetable oil
500g (1lb 2oz) shelled large scallops,
cut into 5mm (¼in) slices
4 celery sticks, sliced diagonally
1 bunch of spring onions,
sliced diagonally
25g (1oz) piece fresh root ginger,
peeled and sliced
2 large garlic cloves, sliced
¼ tsp chilli powder
2 tbsp lemon juice
2 tbsp light soy sauce
3 tbsp freshly chopped coriander
salt and ground black pepper

1 Heat the oil in a wok or large frying pan. Add the scallops, celery, spring onions, ginger, garlic and chilli powder and stir-fry over a high heat for 2 minutes or until the vegetables are just tender.

2 Pour in the lemon juice and soy sauce, allow to bubble up, then stir in about 2 tbsp chopped coriander and season with salt and pepper. Serve immediately, sprinkled with the remaining coriander.

Saffron Paella

Serves 6
Preparation Time
5 minutes
Cooking Time
20 minutes

Per Serving
609 calories
22g fat
(of which 6g saturates)
59g carbohydrate
1.5g salt

Dairy Free

½ tsp saffron threads
900ml–1.1 litres
(1½–2 pints) hot
chicken stock
5 tbsp olive oil
2 × 70g packs sliced
chorizo sausage
6 boneless, skinless
chicken thighs,
each cut into three
pieces
1 large onion, chopped
4 large garlic cloves,
crushed
1 tsp paprika
2 red peppers, seeded
and sliced
400g can chopped

tomatoes in tomato juice
350g (12oz) long-grain
rice
200ml (7fl oz) dry sherry
500g pack ready-
cooked mussels
200g (7oz) cooked tiger
prawns, drained
juice of ½ lemon
salt and ground black
pepper
fresh flat-leafed parsley
sprigs to garnish
(optional)
lemon wedges to serve

1 Add the saffron to the hot stock and leave to infuse for 30 minutes. Meanwhile, heat half the oil in a large heavy-based frying pan. Add half the chorizo and fry for 3–4 minutes until crisp. Remove with a slotted spoon and drain on kitchen paper. Repeat with the remaining chorizo; put to one side.

2 Heat 1 tbsp oil in the pan, add half of the chicken and cook for 3–5 minutes until pale golden brown. Remove from the pan and put to one side. Cook the remaining chicken and put to one side.

3 Reduce the heat slightly, heat the remaining oil and add the onion. Cook for 5 minutes or until soft. Add the garlic and paprika, and cook for 1 minute. Put the chicken back in the pan, then add the peppers and the chopped tomatoes.

4 Stir the rice into the pan, then add a third of the stock and bring to the boil. Season with salt and pepper, reduce the heat and simmer, uncovered, stirring continuously until most of the liquid has been absorbed.

5 Add the remaining stock, a little at a time, allowing the liquid to become absorbed after each addition (this should take about 25 minutes). Add the sherry and cook for a further 2 minutes.

6 Add the mussels and their juices to the pan with the prawns, lemon juice and reserved chorizo. Cook for 5 minutes to heat through. Adjust the seasoning and garnish with parsley sprigs if you like and serve with lemon wedges.

Get Ahead
To prepare ahead Complete to the end of step 3. Cover and keep in a cool place for 1½ hours.
To use Complete the recipe.

Spicy Monkfish Stew

Serves 6
Preparation Time
10 minutes
Cooking Time
35 minutes

Per Serving
142 calories
3g fat
(of which 1g saturates)
16g carbohydrate
0.2g salt

Dairy Free

1 tbsp olive oil
1 onion, finely sliced
1 tbsp tom yum paste (see Cook's Tip)
450g (1lb) potatoes, peeled and cut
into 2cm (¾in) chunks
400g can chopped tomatoes in rich
tomato juice
600ml (1 pint) hot fish stock
450g (1lb) monkfish, cut into 2cm
(¾in) chunks
200g (7oz) ready-to-eat baby spinach
salt and ground black pepper

1 Heat the oil in a pan over a medium heat and fry the onion for 5 minutes until golden.

2 Add the tom yum paste and potatoes, and stir-fry for 1 minute. Add the tomatoes and hot stock, season well with salt and pepper, and cover. Bring to the boil, then reduce the heat and simmer, partially covered, for 15 minutes or until the potatoes are just tender.

3 Add the monkfish to the pan and continue to simmer for 5–10 minutes until the fish is cooked. Add the baby spinach leaves and stir through until wilted.

4 Spoon the fish stew into warmed bowls and serve immediately.

Cook's Tip
Tom yum paste is a hot and spicy Thai mixture used in soups and stews. It is available from large supermarkets and Asian food shops.

Salmon & Bulgur Wheat Pilau

Serves 4

Preparation Time

5 minutes

Cooking Time

20 minutes

Per Serving

323 calories

11g fat

(of which 2g saturates)

30g carbohydrate

1.5g salt

Dairy Free

1 tbsp olive oil
1 onion, chopped
175g (6oz) bulgur wheat
450ml (¾ pint) vegetable stock
400g can pink salmon, drained and flaked
125g (4oz) spinach, roughly chopped
225g (8oz) frozen peas
zest and juice of 1 lemon
salt and ground black pepper

1 Heat the oil in a large pan. Add the onion and cook until softened. Stir in the bulgur wheat to coat in the oil, then stir in the stock and bring to the boil. Cover the pan, reduce the heat and simmer for 10–15 minutes until the stock has been fully absorbed.

2 Stir in the salmon, spinach, peas and lemon juice and cook until the spinach has wilted and the salmon and peas are heated through. Season and sprinkle with lemon zest before serving.

Try Something Different
Instead of salmon, use 200g (7oz) cooked peeled prawns and 200g (7oz) cherry tomatoes.

Chinese-style Fish

Serves 4
Preparation Time
5 minutes
Cooking Time
10 minutes

Per Serving
150 calories
3g fat
(of which 1g saturates)
10g carbohydrate
0.7g salt

Gluten Free Dairy Free

2 tsp sunflower oil
1 small onion, finely chopped
1 green chilli, seeded and finely chopped
(see Cook's Tips, page 10)
2 courgettes, thinly sliced
125g (4oz) frozen peas (defrosted)
350g (12oz) skinless haddock fillet,
cut into bite-size pieces
2 tsp lemon juice
4 tbsp hoisin sauce
lime wedges to serve

1 Heat the oil in a large non-stick frying pan. Add the onion, chilli, courgettes and peas. Stir over a high heat for 5 minutes or until the onion and courgettes begin to soften.

2 Add the fish to the pan with the lemon juice, hoisin sauce and 150ml (¼ pint) water. Bring to the boil, then reduce the heat and simmer, uncovered, for 2–3 minutes until the fish is cooked through. Serve with lime wedges.

Try Something Different
There are plenty of alternatives to haddock: try sea bass, sea bream or gurnard.

Stir-fried Salmon & Broccoli

Serves 2
Preparation Time
10 minutes
Cooking Time
5–6 minutes

Per Serving
90 calories
4g fat
(of which 1g saturates)
9g carbohydrate
2.7g salt

Dairy Free

2 tsp sesame oil
1 red pepper, seeded and thinly sliced
½ red chilli, thinly sliced (see Cook's
Tips, page 10)
1 garlic clove, crushed
125g (4oz) broccoli florets
2 spring onions, sliced
2 salmon fillets, about 125g (4oz) each,
cut into strips
1 tsp Thai fish sauce
2 tsp soy sauce
wholewheat noodles to serve

1 Heat the oil in a wok or large frying pan. Add the red
pepper, chilli, garlic, broccoli florets and spring
onions. Stir-fry over a high heat for 3–4 minutes.

2 Add the salmon, fish sauce and soy sauce and cook
for 2 minutes, stirring gently. Serve immediately with
wholewheat noodles.

Moules Marinière

Serves 4
Preparation Time
15 minutes
Cooking Time
20 minutes

Per Serving
266 calories
13g fat
(of which 7g saturates)
2g carbohydrate
0.9g salt

Gluten Free

2kg (4½lb) fresh mussels, scrubbed, rinsed and beards removed (see Cook's Tips)
25g (1oz) butter
4 shallots, finely chopped
2 garlic cloves, crushed
200ml (7fl oz) dry white wine
2 tbsp freshly chopped flat-leafed parsley
100ml (3½fl oz) single cream
salt and ground black pepper
crusty bread to serve

1 Tap the mussels on the worksurface, and discard any that do not close or have broken shells. Heat the butter in a large non-stick lidded frying pan, and sauté the shallots over a medium-high heat for about 10 minutes until soft.

2 Add the garlic, wine and half the parsley to the pan, and bring to the boil. Tip in the mussels and reduce the heat a little. Cover and cook for about 5 minutes or until all the shells have opened; discard any mussels that don't open.

3 Lift out the mussels with a slotted spoon and put into serving bowls, and cover with foil to keep warm. Add the cream to the stock, season with salt and pepper, and cook for 1–2 minutes to heat through.

4 Pour a little sauce over the mussels and sprinkle with the rest of the chopped parsley. Serve immediately with crusty bread.

Cook's Tips
To prepare fresh mussels, rinse them under cold running water, scrub the shells thoroughly to remove any barnacles then pull off the hairy beard. Tap any open mussels sharply with the back of the knife and if they refuse to close discard.
To make sure mussels are safe to eat, check them carefully for cracks and split shells before cooking. Discard these, and any that do not close when tapped sharply. Any mussels that remain closed after cooking should also be thrown away.

Haddock & Tomato Casserole

Serves 4

Preparation Time
15 minutes

Cooking Time
50 minutes

Per Serving
307 calories
9g fat
(of which 1g saturates)
27g carbohydrate
0.4g salt

2 tbsp olive oil
4 shallots, finely chopped
1 leek, finely sliced
2 medium potatoes, about 400g (14oz),
cut into 1cm (½ in) pieces
150ml (¼ pint) white wine
2 x 400g can chopped tomatoes
1½ tsp dried oregano
pinch of sugar
4 x 125g (4oz) haddock or other white fish
fillets, skinned
salt and pepper
large handful fresh basil, roughly chopped

1 Heat half the oil in a large, hob-proof casserole and gently fry the shallots and leek for 5-8 minutes until softened. Add the potato and pour in the wine. Bubble for 2-3 minutes.

2 Stir in the chopped tomatoes, oregano, sugar, a little seasoning and 150ml (¼ pint) water. Simmer for 35 minutes, stirring occasionally, until the potatoes are tender.

3 Season the fish fillets and nestle them into the stew. Cover the pan and simmer gently for 5 minutes until the fish is cooked through. Stir gently to flake the fish, then check the seasoning. Sprinkle with basil and serve immediately.

Spanish Fish Stew

Serves 4
Preparation Time
20 minutes
Cooking Time
1 hour 10 minutes

Per Serving
463 calories
22g fat
(of which 6g saturates)
32g carbohydrate
1.8g salt

Gluten Free Dairy Free

350g (12oz) small salad potatoes, halved
175g (6oz) chorizo sausage, skinned and
roughly chopped
350g jar roasted peppers in olive oil,
drained and chopped, oil reserved
1 garlic clove, crushed
2 small red onions, cut into thick wedges
175ml (6fl oz) dry white wine
300g (11oz) passata
25g (1oz) pitted black olives
450g (1lb) chunky white fish, such as
cod and haddock, cut into large cubes
salt and ground black pepper
freshly chopped flat-leafed parsley to
garnish

1 Preheat the oven to 170°C (150°C fan oven) mark 3.
Put the potatoes, chorizo, roasted peppers, garlic,
onions, wine and passata into a large flameproof
casserole with 2 tbsp of the oil from the peppers. Season
with salt and pepper.

2 Bring to the boil over a medium heat, then cover with
a tight-fitting lid and cook in the oven for 45 minutes.

3 Add the olives and fish, and put back in the oven for
15 minutes or until the fish is opaque and completely
cooked through. Spoon into warmed bowls and serve
garnished with chopped parsley.

Cook's Tip
Passata is a useful storecupboard ingredient from the
Italian kitchen, which can be used in sauces and stews.
It is made from ripe tomatoes that have been puréed
and sieved to make a very smooth sauce.

Easy Thai Red Chicken Curry

Serves 4

Preparation Time
5 minutes

Cooking Time
20 minutes

Per Serving
248 calories
8g fat
(of which 1g saturates)
16g carbohydrate
1g salt

Dairy Free

1 tbsp vegetable oil
3 tbsp Thai red curry paste
4 skinless chicken breasts, around 600g
(1lb 5oz), sliced
400ml can coconut milk
300ml (½ pint) hot chicken or vegetable stock
juice of 1 lime
200g pack mixed baby sweetcorn and mangetouts
2 tbsp freshly chopped coriander
lime wedges and rice or rice noodles to serve

1 Heat the oil in a wok or large pan over a low heat. Add the curry paste and cook for 2 minutes until it is fragrant.

2 Add the sliced chicken and fry gently for about 10 minutes until browned.

3 Add the coconut milk, hot stock, lime juice and baby corn to the pan and bring to the boil. Add the mangetouts, then reduce the heat and simmer for 4–5 minutes or until the chicken is cooked. Add the chopped coriander and serve immediately with lime wedges and rice or noodles.

Throw-it-all-together Chicken Salad

Serves 4
Preparation Time
10 minutes

Per Serving
215 calories
9g fat
(of which 2g saturates)
9g carbohydrate
0.6g salt

Gluten Free Dairy Free

4 chargrilled chicken breasts,
about 125g (4oz) each, torn into strips
2 carrots, cut into strips
½ cucumber, halved lengthways,
seeded and cut into ribbons
a handful of fresh coriander leaves,
roughly chopped
½ head of Chinese leaves, shredded
4 handfuls of watercress
4 spring onions, shredded

For the dressing
5 tbsp peanut butter
2 tbsp sweet chilli sauce
juice of 1 lime
salt and ground black pepper

1 Put the chicken strips and all the salad ingredients into a large salad bowl.

2 To make the dressing, put the peanut butter, chilli sauce and lime juice into a small bowl and mix well. Season with salt and pepper. If the dressing is too thick to pour, add 2-3 tbsp cold water, a tablespoon at a time, to thin it – use just enough water to make the dressing the correct consistency.

3 Drizzle the dressing over the salad, toss gently together and serve.

Cook's Tips
Use leftover roast chicken or beef, or cooked ham for this recipe.
Use washed and prepared salad instead of Chinese leaves and watercress.

One-pan Chicken with Tomatoes

Serves 4
Preparation Time
5 minutes
Cooking Time
20–25 minutes

Per Serving
238 calories
4g fat
(of which 1g saturates)
20g carbohydrate
1g salt

Gluten Free Dairy Free

4 chicken thighs
1 red onion, sliced
400g can chopped tomatoes with herbs
400g can mixed beans, drained and rinsed
2 tsp balsamic vinegar
salt and ground black pepper
freshly chopped flat-leafed parsley to garnish

1 Heat a non-stick pan and fry the chicken thighs, skin side down, until golden. Turn over and fry for 5 minutes.

2 Add the onion and fry for 5 minutes. Add the tomatoes, mixed beans and vinegar, cover the pan and simmer for 10–12 minutes until piping hot. Check the seasoning. Garnish with parsley and serve immediately.

Try Something Different
Use flageolet beans or other canned beans instead of mixed beans, and garnish with fresh basil or oregano.

Chicken Cacciatore

Serves 4
Preparation Time
5 minutes
Cooking Time
40 minutes

Per Serving
327 calories
17g fat
(of which 4g saturates)
3g carbohydrate
1.3g salt

Gluten Free Dairy Free

2 tbsp olive oil
8 boneless, skinless chicken thighs
2 garlic cloves, crushed
1 tsp dried thyme
1 tsp dried tarragon
150ml (¼ pint) white wine
400g can chopped tomatoes
12 pitted black olives
12 capers, rinsed and drained
ground black pepper
brown rice and broad beans or peas to serve

1 Heat the oil in a flameproof casserole over a high heat. Add the chicken and brown all over. Reduce the heat and add the garlic, thyme, tarragon and wine to the casserole. Stir for 1 minute, then add the tomatoes and season with pepper.

2 Bring to the boil, then reduce the heat, cover the casserole and simmer for 20 minutes or until the chicken is tender.

3 Lift the chicken out of the casserole and put to one side. Bubble the sauce for 5 minutes or until thickened, add the olives and capers, stir well and cook for a further 2–3 minutes.

4 Put the chicken into the sauce. Serve with brown rice and broad beans or peas.

Chicken & Gruyère Salad

Serves 8
Preparation Time
15 minutes,
plus chilling

Per Serving
507 calories
40g fat
(of which 9g saturates)
7g carbohydrate
0.7g salt

Gluten Free

900g–1kg (2–2¼lb) cooked, boned chicken, skinned and cut into bite-size pieces
4 celery sticks, thinly sliced
125g (4oz) Gruyère or Emmenthal cheese, coarsely grated
2 firm red apples, halved, cored and roughly chopped
125g (4oz) seedless black grapes, halved
200ml (7fl oz) olive oil
2 tbsp white wine vinegar
4 tbsp soured cream
4 tbsp mayonnaise
4 tbsp freshly chopped parsley
75g (3oz) toasted pecan nuts or walnuts
salt and ground black pepper
chopped coriander and rocket to serve

1 Put the chicken, celery, cheese, apples and grapes into a large bowl. Add all the other ingredients and toss well.

2 Adjust the seasoning, cover and leave to chill in the fridge for at least 10–15 minutes. Serve with chopped coriander scattered over the top and rocket.

Cook's Tips
Any strongly flavoured cheese can be used for this recipe. You could try crumbled Danish blue or blue Stilton. The whole salad can be completed the day before and kept covered in the fridge until required. Stir well before serving.

Chicken Tagine with Apricots & Almonds

Serves 4
Preparation Time
10 minutes
Cooking Time
about 1 hour

Per Serving
376 calories
22g fat
(of which 4g saturates)
19g carbohydrate
0.5g salt

Dairy Free

2 tbsp olive oil
4 chicken thighs
1 onion, chopped
2 tsp ground cinnamon
2 tbsp runny honey
150g (5oz) dried apricots
75g (3oz) blanched almonds
250ml (9fl oz) hot chicken stock
salt and ground black pepper
flaked almonds to garnish
couscous to serve

1 Heat 1 tbsp of the oil in a large flameproof casserole over a medium heat. Add the chicken and fry for 5 minutes until brown. Remove from the casserole and put to one side to keep warm.

2 Add the onion to the pan with the remaining olive oil and fry for 10 minutes until softened.

3 Put the chicken back in the pan with the cinnamon, honey, apricots, almonds and hot stock. Season well, stir once, then cover and bring to the boil. Reduce the heat and simmer for 45 minutes or until the chicken is falling off the bone.

4 Garnish the tagine with flaked almonds and serve hot with couscous.

Chicken, Bean & Spinach Curry

Serves 4
Preparation Time
10 minutes
Cooking Time
about 20 minutes

Per Serving
364 calories
9g fat
(of which 1g saturates)
41g carbohydrate
2.9g salt

Gluten Free

1 tbsp sunflower oil
350g (12oz) skinless chicken breasts,
cut into strips
1 garlic clove, crushed
300–350g tub or jar curry sauce
400g can aduki beans, drained and rinsed
175g (6oz) ready-to-eat dried apricots
150g (5oz) natural bio yogurt
125g (4oz) ready-to-eat baby spinach
naan bread to serve

1 Heat the oil in a large pan over a medium heat, and
fry the chicken strips with the garlic until golden.
Add the curry sauce, aduki beans and apricots, then
cover and simmer gently for 15 minutes or until the
chicken is tender.

2 Over a low heat, stir in the yogurt, keeping the curry
hot without boiling it, then stir in the spinach until it
just begins to wilt. Serve immediately with naan bread.

Try Something Different
Use pork escalopes cut into thin strips instead of chicken.

Spicy Sausage & Pasta Supper

Serves 6
Preparation Time
15 minutes
Cooking Time
30 minutes

Per Serving
629 calories
39g fat
(of which 18g saturates)
36g carbohydrate
3.1g salt

1 tbsp olive oil
200g (7oz) salami, sliced
225g (8oz) onion, finely chopped
50g (2oz) celery, finely chopped
2 garlic cloves, crushed
400g can pimientos, drained, rinsed and chopped
400g (14oz) passata or 400g can chopped tomatoes
125g (4oz) sun-dried tomatoes in oil, drained
600ml (1 pint) hot chicken or vegetable stock

300ml (½ pint) red wine
1 tbsp sugar
75g (3oz) dried pasta shapes
400g can borlotti beans, drained and rinsed
salt and ground black pepper
freshly chopped flat-leafed parsley to garnish
300ml (½ pint) soured cream and 175g (6oz) Parmesan, freshly grated, to serve

1 Heat the oil in a large pan over a medium heat and fry the salami for 5 minutes or until golden and crisp. Drain on kitchen paper.

2 Fry the onion and celery in the hot oil for 10 minutes or until soft and golden. Add the garlic and fry for 1 minute. Put the salami back in the pan with the pimientos, passata or chopped tomatoes, sun-dried tomatoes, hot stock, red wine and sugar. Bring to the boil.

3 Stir in the pasta, bring back to the boil and cook for about 10 minutes or according to the packet instructions until the pasta is almost tender.

4 Stir in the beans and simmer for 3–4 minutes. Top up with more stock if the pasta is not tender when the liquid has been absorbed. Season with salt and pepper.

5 Ladle into warmed bowls and serve topped with soured cream and garnished with the chopped parsley. Serve the grated Parmesan separately.

Get Ahead
To prepare ahead Complete the recipe to the end of step 2, cool quickly, cover and chill for up to one day.
To use Bring back to the boil, stir in the pasta and complete the recipe.

Salami & Olive Tart

Serves 6
Preparation Time
10 minutes
Cooking Time
25 minutes

Per Serving
370 calories
28g fat
(of which 1g saturates)
25g carbohydrate
1.4g salt

375g pack ready-rolled puff pastry
4 tbsp chargrilled aubergine pesto
12 slices Italian salami, thinly sliced
(about 70g/scant 3oz)
2 medium tomatoes, sliced
2 tbsp pitted black olives, sliced
2 large handfuls of rocket
extra virgin olive oil for drizzling

1 Preheat the oven to 200°C (180°C fan oven) mark 6.
Unroll the pastry and put on a baking sheet, then fold
the edges over by 1cm (½in) as a border. Prick the base
all over with a fork.

2 Spread the pesto over the base inside the border.
Arrange the salami and tomatoes in overlapping
layers on top. Bake for 20–25 minutes until golden.
Garnish with the olives, rocket and a drizzle of olive oil
to serve.

One-pot Gammon Stew

Serves 4
Preparation Time
15 minutes
Cooking Time
1 hour 10 minutes

Per Serving
680 calories
30g fat
(of which 11g saturates)
41g carbohydrate
6.3g salt

Gluten Free

1 tbsp olive oil
1.1kg (2½lb) smoked gammon joint
8 shallots, blanched in boiling water,
drained, peeled and chopped into chunks
3 carrots, chopped into chunks
3 celery sticks, chopped into chunks
4 large Desiree potatoes, unpeeled
450ml (¾ pint) each apple juice and hot
vegetable stock
½ small Savoy cabbage
25g (1oz) butter

1 Preheat the oven to 190°C (170°C fan oven) mark 5.
Heat the oil in a large flameproof casserole. Add the
gammon and cook for 5 minutes or until brown all over.
Remove from the pan.

2 Add the shallots, carrots and celery to the pan and fry
for 3–4 minutes until starting to soften.

3 Return the gammon to the pan. Chop the potatoes
into quarters and add to the pan with the apple juice
and hot stock. Cover and bring to the boil, then transfer
to the oven and cook for 50 minutes or until the meat is
cooked through and the vegetables are tender.

4 Remove from the oven and put the dish back on the
hob over a low heat. Shred the cabbage and stir into
the pan. Simmer for 2–3 minutes, then stir in the butter
and serve.

Spanish-style Pork

Serves 4

Preparation Time
15 minutes

Cooking Time
25 minutes

Per Serving
349 calories
12g fat
(of which 3g saturates)
26g carbohydrate
1.2g salt

Dairy Free

500g (1lb 2oz) pork fillet, trimmed and sliced
2 tbsp olive oil
1 Spanish onion, chopped
2 celery sticks, finely chopped
2 tsp smoked paprika
1 tbsp tomato purée
750ml (1¼ pints) hot chicken stock
400g can butter beans, drained and rinsed
¼ Savoy cabbage, finely shredded
200g (7oz) green beans, trimmed and halved
salt and ground black pepper
1 tbsp freshly chopped rosemary to garnish
lemon wedges and crusty bread to serve

1 Lay the pork out on a board, cover with clingfilm and flatten slightly with a rolling pin. Heat 1 tbsp oil in a frying pan and fry the pork over a medium–high heat until browned. Remove from the pan and set aside.

2 Heat the remaining oil and gently fry the chopped onion and celery for 10 minutes or until softened. Stir in the paprika and tomato purée and cook for 1 minute. Stir in the hot stock, butter beans and cabbage. Season with salt and pepper.

3 Return the pork to the pan and bring to the boil, then reduce the heat and simmer for 10 minutes, adding the green beans for the last 4 minutes. Garnish with rosemary and serve with lemon wedges and crusty bread on the side.

Ribs & Beans in a Sticky Barbecue Sauce

Serves 4
Preparation Time
10 minutes
Cooking time
1¼ hours

Per serving
620 calories
25g fat
(of which 10g saturates)
53g carbohydrate
1g salt

8 meaty pork spare ribs
1 large onion, chopped
2 large garlic cloves, chopped
4 tbsp light muscovado sugar
1 tbsp French mustard
4 tbsp sun-dried tomato paste
150g (5oz) passata
4 tbsp malt vinegar
4 tbsp tomato ketchup
2 tbsp Worcestershire sauce
568ml can dry cider
2 × 410g cans black-eye beans,
drained and rinsed
salt and ground black pepper
4 tbsp freshly chopped parsley
to garnish

1 Trim the spare ribs of excess fat if necessary and season with salt and pepper.

2 Put the onion, garlic, sugar, mustard, tomato paste, passata, vinegar, ketchup and Worcestershire sauce into a large roasting tin and stir well. Add the spare ribs and stir to coat in the sauce.

3 Cook in the oven at 210°C (190°C fan oven) mark 6½ for 30 minutes, then turn the ribs over and cook for a further 30 minutes until they are crisp and brown.

4 Add the cider and stir to mix well with the sauce, scraping up the sediment from the bottom of the pan. Add the black-eye beans, stir and return to the oven for a further 15 minutes. Scatter with chopped parsley to garnish and serve.

Try Something Different
Use canned haricot or pinto beans instead of the black-eye beans.

One-pot Spicy Beef

Serves 4
Preparation Time
10 minutes
Cooking Time
40 minutes

Per Serving
487 calories
21g fat
(of which 8g saturates)
45g carbohydrate,1.8g
salt

Gluten Free Dairy Free

2 tsp sunflower oil
1 large onion, roughly chopped
1 garlic clove, finely chopped
1 small fresh red chilli, finely chopped
(see Cook's Tips, page 10)
2 red peppers, roughly chopped
2 celery sticks, diced
400g (14oz) lean beef mince
400g can chopped tomatoes
2 × 400g cans mixed beans, drained
and rinsed
1–2 tsp Tabasco sauce
2–3 tbsp roughly chopped fresh
coriander to garnish (optional)
salsa (see Cook's Tip) and soft flour
tortillas or basmati rice to serve

1 Heat the oil in a large heavy-based frying pan over a medium heat. Add the onion to the pan with 2 tbsp water. Cook for 10 minutes or until soft. Add the garlic and chilli, and cook for a further 1–2 minutes until golden. Add the red peppers and celery, and cook for 5 minutes.

2 Add the beef to the pan and brown all over. Add the tomatoes, beans and Tabasco sauce, then simmer for 20 minutes. Garnish with coriander, if you like, and serve with salsa and tortillas or rice.

Cook's Tip
To make a quick salsa, peel and roughly chop ½ ripe avocado. Put in a bowl with 4 roughly chopped tomatoes, 1 tsp olive oil and the juice of ½ lime. Mix well.

Lamb & Pasta Pot

Serves 4
Preparation Time
10 minutes
Cooking Time
50 minutes

Per Serving
686 calories
36g fat
(of which 16g saturates)
18g carbohydrate
1.4g salt

Dairy Free

1 half leg of lamb roasting joint –
about 1.1kg (2½lb) total weight
125g (4oz) smoked streaky bacon,
chopped
150ml (¼ pint) red wine
400g can chopped tomatoes with
chilli, or 400g (14oz) passata
75g (3oz) pasta shapes
12 sunblush tomatoes
150g (5oz) chargrilled artichokes in
oil, drained and halved
a handful of basil leaves to garnish

1 Preheat the oven to 200°C (180°C fan oven) mark 6.
Put the lamb and bacon into a small deep roasting
tin and fry for 5 minutes or until the lamb is brown all
over and the bacon is beginning to crisp.

2 Remove the lamb and put to one side. Pour the wine
into the tin with the bacon – it should bubble
immediately. Stir well, scraping the bottom of the tin to
loosen any crusty bits, then leave to bubble until half the
wine has evaporated. Stir in 300ml (½ pint) water and
add the chopped tomatoes or passata, the pasta and
sunblush tomatoes.

3 Put the lamb on a rack over the roasting tin so that
the juices drip into the pasta. Cook, uncovered, in the
oven for about 35 minutes.

4 Stir the artichokes into the pasta and put everything
back in the oven for 5 minutes or until the lamb is
tender and the pasta cooked. Slice the lamb thickly and
serve with the pasta, garnished with the basil.

Turkish Lamb Stew

Serves 4
Preparation Time
10 minutes
Cooking Time
about 2 hours

Per Serving
389 calories
20g fat
(of which 7g saturates)
28g carbohydrate
1.2g salt

Gluten Free Dairy Free

2 tbsp olive oil
400g (14oz) lean lamb fillet, cubed
1 red onion, sliced
1 garlic clove, crushed
1 potato, quartered
400g can chopped plum tomatoes
1 red pepper, seeded and sliced
200g (7oz) canned chickpeas,
drained and rinsed
1 aubergine, cut into chunks
200ml (7fl oz) lamb stock
1 tbsp red wine vinegar
1 tsp each freshly chopped thyme,
rosemary and oregano
8 black olives, halved and pitted
salt and ground black pepper

1 Heat 1 tbsp oil in a large flameproof casserole and brown the lamb over a high heat. Reduce the heat and add the remaining oil, the onion and garlic, then cook until soft.

2 Preheat the oven to 170°C (150°C fan oven) mark 3. Add the potato, tomatoes, red pepper, chickpeas, aubergine, stock, vinegar and herbs to the pan. Season, stir and bring to the boil. Cover the pan, transfer to the oven and cook for 1–1½ hours until the lamb is tender.

3 About 15 minutes before the end of the cooking time, add the olives.

Spiced Nectarines

Serves 4
Preparation Time
10 minutes, plus
cooling

Per Serving
95 calories
trace fat, 23g
carbohydrate
0g salt

Vegetarian
Gluten Free

4 tbsp clear honey
2 star anise
1 tbsp lemon juice
4 ripe nectarines or peaches, halved and stoned
cream or vanilla ice cream to serve

1 Put the honey, star anise and lemon juice into a heatproof bowl. Stir in 150ml (¼ pint) boiling water and leave until just warm.

2 Add the nectarines to the warm honey syrup and leave to cool. Serve with cream or vanilla ice cream.

Try Something Different
Use a cinnamon stick instead of the star anise.

Spiced Winter Fruit

Serves 6
Preparation Time
20 minutes, plus
cooling
Cooking Time
20 minutes

Per Serving
207 calories
trace fat, 45g
carbohydrate
0g salt

Vegetarian
Gluten Free Dairy Free

50g (2oz) large muscatel raisins or dried
blueberries
1 small pineapple, peeled, cored and thinly sliced
1 mango, peeled, stoned and thickly sliced
3 tangerines, peeled and halved horizontally
3 fresh figs, halved

For the syrup
150ml (¼ pint) port
150ml (¼ pint) freshly squeezed orange juice
75g (3oz) light muscovado sugar
1 cinnamon stick
6 cardamom pods, lightly crushed
5cm (2in) piece fresh root ginger, peeled and
thinly sliced

1 First, make the syrup. Pour the port and orange juice
into a small pan, then add the sugar and 300ml
(½ pint) cold water. Bring to the boil, stirring all the time.
Add the cinnamon stick, cardamom pods and ginger,
then bubble gently for 15 minutes.

2 Put all the fruit into a serving bowl. Remove the
cinnamon stick and cardamom pods from the syrup –
or leave in for a spicier flavour – then pour the syrup over
the fruit. Serve warm or cold.

Baked Apricots with Almonds

Serves 6
Preparation Time
5 minutes
Cooking Time
20-25 minutes

Per Serving
124 calories
6g fat
(of which 2g saturates)
16g carbohydrate
0.1g salt

Vegetarian Gluten Free Dairy Free

12 apricots, halved and stoned
3 tbsp golden caster sugar
2 tbsp amaretto liqueur
25g (1oz) unsalted butter
25g (1oz) flaked almonds
crème fraîche to serve

1 Preheat the oven to 200°C (180°C fan oven) mark 6. Put the apricot halves, cut side up, into an ovenproof dish. Sprinkle with the sugar, drizzle with the liqueur, then dot each apricot half with a little butter. Scatter the flaked almonds over them.

2 Bake in the oven for 20-25 minutes until the apricots are soft and the juices are syrupy. Serve warm, with crème fraîche.

Try Something Different
Use nectarines or peaches instead of apricots.

Apple Tart

Serves 8
Preparation Time
10 minutes
Cooking Time
20–25 minutes

Per Serving
221 calories
12g fat
(of which 0g saturates)
29g carbohydrate
0.4g salt

Vegetarian

375g packet all-butter ready-rolled puff pastry
500g (1lb 2oz) Cox's apples, cored, thinly sliced
and tossed in the juice of 1 lemon
golden icing sugar to dust

1 Preheat the oven to 200°C (180°C fan oven) mark 6. Put the pastry on a 28 × 38cm (11 × 15in) baking sheet, and roll lightly with a rolling pin to smooth down the pastry. Score lightly around the edge, to create a 3cm (1¼in) border.

2 Put the apple slices on top of the pastry, within the border. Turn the edge of the pastry halfway over, so that it reaches the edge of the apples, then press down and use your fingers to crimp the edge. Dust heavily with icing sugar.

3 Bake in the oven for 20–25 minutes until the pastry is cooked and the sugar has caramelised. Serve warm, dusted with more icing sugar.

Drunken Pears

Serves 4
Preparation Time
15 minutes
Cooking Time
50 minutes

Per Serving
305 calories
trace fat, 52g
carbohydrate
0g salt

Vegetarian
Gluten Free Dairy Free

4 Williams or Comice pears
150g (5oz) granulated sugar
300ml (½ pint) red wine
150ml (¼ pint) sloe gin
1 cinnamon stick
zest of 1 orange
6 star anise
Greek yogurt or whipped cream
to serve (optional)

1 Peel the pears, cut out the calyx at the base of each and leave the stalks intact. Put the sugar, wine, sloe gin and 300ml (½ pint) water into a small pan and heat gently until the sugar dissolves.

2 Bring to the boil and add the cinnamon stick, orange zest and star anise. Add the pears, then cover and poach over a low heat for 30 minutes or until tender.

3 Remove the pears with a slotted spoon, then continue to heat the liquid until it has reduced to about 200ml (7fl oz) or until syrupy. Pour the syrup over the pears. Serve warm or chilled with Greek yogurt or whipped cream, if you like.

Get Ahead
To prepare ahead Complete the recipe, cool, cover and chill for up to three days.

Peach Brûlée

Serves 4
Preparation Time
10 minutes
Cooking Time
about 10 minutes

Per Serving
137 calories
6g fat
(of which 4g saturates)
21g carbohydrate
0.1g salt

Vegetarian
Gluten Free

4 ripe peaches, halved and stone removed
8 tsp soft cream cheese
8 tsp golden caster sugar

1 Preheat the grill until very hot. Fill each stone cavity in the fruit with 2 tsp cream cheese, then sprinkle each one with 2 tsp caster sugar.

2 Put the fruit halves on a grill pan, and cook under the very hot grill until the sugar has browned and caramelised to create a brûlée crust. Serve warm.

Try Something Different
Use nectarines instead of peaches.

Poached Plums with Port

Serves 4
Preparation Time
5 minutes
Cooking Time
20 minutes

Per Serving
97 calories
0g fat, 23g
carbohydrate
0g salt

Vegetarian
Gluten Free Dairy Free

75g (3oz) golden caster sugar
2 tbsp port
6 large plums, halved and stoned
1 cinnamon stick
vanilla ice cream to serve (optional)

1 Put the sugar in a pan with 500ml (18fl oz) water. Heat gently until the sugar dissolves. Bring to the boil, reduce the heat and simmer rapidly for 2 minutes without stirring.

2 Stir in the port. Add the plums to the pan with the cinnamon stick, and simmer gently for 5–10 minutes until the fruit is tender but still keeping its shape.

3 Remove the plums and put to one side, discarding the cinnamon. Simmer the syrup until it has reduced by two-thirds. Serve the plums warm or cold, drizzled with syrup and with a scoop of vanilla ice cream alongside, if you like.

Rice Pudding

Serves 6
Preparation Time
5 minutes
Cooking Time
1½ hours

Per Serving
235 calories
7g fat
(of which 5g saturates)
35g carbohydrate
0.2g salt

Vegetarian
Gluten Free

butter to grease
125g (4oz) short-grain pudding rice
1.1 litres (2 pints) full-fat milk
4 tbsp golden caster sugar
grated zest of 1 small orange
2 tsp vanilla extract
whole nutmeg to grate

1 Preheat the oven to 180°C (160°C fan oven) mark 4. Lightly butter a 900ml (1½ pint) ovenproof dish. Add the pudding rice, milk, sugar, orange zest and vanilla extract, and stir everything together. Grate a little nutmeg all over the top of the mixture.

2 Bake the pudding in the oven for 1½ hours or until the top is golden brown, then serve.

Fruity Rice Pudding

Serves 6
Preparation Time
10 minutes, plus
cooling and chilling
Cooking Time
1 hour

Per Serving
323 calories
17g fat
(of which 10g saturates)
36g carbohydrate
0.2g salt

Vegetarian
Gluten Free

125g (4oz) pudding rice
1.1 litres (2 pints) full-fat milk
1 tsp vanilla extract
3–4 tbsp caster sugar
200ml (7fl oz) whipping cream
6 tbsp wild lingonberry sauce

1 Put the rice into a pan with 600ml (1 pint) cold water and bring to the boil, then reduce the heat and simmer until the liquid has evaporated. Add the milk and bring to the boil, then reduce the heat and simmer for 45 minutes or until the rice is very soft and creamy. Leave to cool.

2 Add the vanilla extract and sugar to the rice. Lightly whip the cream and fold through the pudding. Chill for 1 hour.

3 Divide the rice mixture among six glass dishes and top with 1 tbsp lingonberry sauce.

Try Something Different
Although wild lingonberry sauce is used here, a spoonful of any fruit sauce or compote such as strawberry or blueberry will taste delicious.
For an alternative presentation, serve in tumblers, layering the rice pudding with the fruit sauce; you will need to use double the amount of fruit sauce.

Rich Chocolate Pots

Serves 6
Preparation Time
10 minutes, plus
chilling
Cooking Time
10 minutes

Per Serving
895 calories
66g fat
(of which 41g saturates)
66g carbohydrate
0g salt
Gluten Free

300g (11oz) plain chocolate
(at least 70% cocoa solids),
broken into pieces
300ml (½ pint) double cream
250g (9oz) mascarpone cheese
3 tbsp cognac
1 tbsp vanilla extract
6 tbsp crème fraîche
chocolate curls to decorate
(see Cook's Tip)

1 Melt the plain chocolate in a heatproof bowl set over a pan of gently simmering water. Remove the bowl from the heat and add the cream, mascarpone, cognac and vanilla extract. Mix well – the hot chocolate will melt into the cream and mascarpone.

2 Divide the mixture among six 150ml (¼ pint) glasses and chill for 20 minutes. Spoon some crème fraîche on top of each chocolate pot and decorate with the chocolate curls.

Cook's Tip

Chocolate Curls Melt the chocolate in a heatproof bowl set over a pan of simmering water. Spread it out in a thin layer on a marble slab or clean worksurface. Leave to firm up. Using a sharp blade (such as a pastry scraper, a cook's knife or a very stiff spatula), draw it through the chocolate at a 45° angle. The size of the curls will be determined by the width of the blade.

Index

KITCHEN NOTES

Both metric and imperial measures are given for the recipes. Follow either set of measures, not a mixture of both, as they are not interchangeable.

All spoon measures are level.
1 tsp = 5ml spoon; 1 tbsp = 15ml spoon.

Ovens and grills must be preheated to the specified temperature.

Medium eggs should be used except where otherwise specified. Free-range eggs are recommended.

Note that some recipes contain raw or lightly cooked eggs. The young, elderly, pregnant women and anyone with an immune-deficiency disease should avoid these because of the slight risk of salmonella.

Photographers: Neil Barclay (pages 63 and 70); Martin Brigdale (pages 22, 23, 44, 45 and 52); Nicki Dowey (pages 5, 8, 9, 12, 13, 14, 15, 16, 17, 18, 30, 31, 33, 35, 38, 39, 48, 49, 50, 51, 54, 56, 62, 71, 79, 80, 81, 82, 83, 88, 89 and 93); Will Heap (pages 19, 66 and 67); Gareth Morgans page 55; Craig Robertson (pages 6, 7, 10, 11, 20, 21, 24, 25, 26, 27, 28, 29, 32, 34, 36, 37, 42, 43, 46, 47, 53, 57, 58, 59, 60, 61, 68, 69, 72, 73, 76, 77, 78, 84, 85, 86, 87, 90, 91, 92 and 94); Lucinda Symons (pages 40, 41, 64 and 65); Martin Thompson (pages 74 and 75).

Cover photograph: Gareth Morgans
Home Economists: Joanna Farrow, Emma Jane Frost, Teresa Goldfinch, Alice Hart, Lucy McKelvie, Kim Morphew, Aya Nishimura, Bridget Sargeson, Kate Trend and Mari Mererid Williams.
Stylists: Tamzin Ferdinando, Wei Tang, Helen Trent and Fanny Ward.

First published in Great Britain in 2012
by Collins & Brown
10 Southcombe Street
London W14 0RA

An imprint of Anova Books Company Ltd

The Good Housekeeping website is
www.allaboutyou.com/goodhousekeeping

ISBN 978-1-908449-29-0

A catalogue record for this book is available from the British Library.

Reproduction by Dot Gradations Ltd, UK
Printed and bound by 1010 Printing International Ltd, China

This book can be ordered direct from the publisher. Contact the marketing department, but try your bookshop first.

www.anovabooks.com